*Flying high at the popular annual
Kite Festival hosted by the Cape Mental
Health Society, Muizenberg.*

DOUBLE
STOREY
a juta company

Cape Town
uncovered
A PEOPLE'S CITY

Gillian Warren-Brown and Yazeed Fakier

Photographs by Eric Miller

Tourists are a curiosity everywhere, even on tours of the townships.

Published 2005 by Double Storey Books,
a division of Juta & Co. Ltd, Mercury Crescent, Wetton, Cape Town

© 2005 text Gillian Warren-Brown & Yazeed Fakier; photographs Eric Miller

ISBN 1 919930 75 2

Editing by Sandy Shepherd
Text design and layout by Jenny Young
Cover design by Jenny Young
Scans by Colour Studio
Printing by Pacifica Communications, Korea

Our thanks to Andrew Boraine and the numerous other people who gave their time and energy towards the creation of this book. Thanks, also, to Creative Colour for sponsoring film processing.

Previous page: Still glowing after receiving their matric results earlier in the day, Clifton Beach.

Contents

Celebrating Women's Day, Langa.

Cape Town Uncovered

It's not easy to produce a book about Cape Town – this impossibly beautiful city with so many natural attractions, alongside large areas of social deprivation. Cape Town – a city internationally famous for its mountains, beaches and vineyards, and, at the same time, a city not yet in possession of a common identity for its people.

How do you capture the contradictions? How do you promote Cape Town, with all its fabulous places and destinations, and remain honest about the scale of the inequalities and development challenges?

Cape Town Uncovered: A People's City bravely seeks to do just that, and succeeds. It is not a sociology textbook; neither is it a glossy coffee-table publication throwing clichés at tourists. *Cape Town Uncovered* delves into the character of the city by focusing on its people and their cultures, occupations, activities and dreams, rather than on conventional icons.

It does this firstly through Eric Miller's beautiful and sensitive images of Capetonians, portraits of diversity without the traditional sentimentality. Then there's the text by Gillian Warren-Brown and Yazeed Fakier. From Ebrahim Manuel's amazing journey of discovery of his roots in Indonesia and Elizabeth Mitchell's tragic story of forced removal from Tramway Road in Sea Point, to the uplifting story of Thandumzi Moyakhe and the Dance for All programme, *Cape Town Uncovered* introduces us to the (often hidden) histories, religions, food, music and languages of the people of Cape Town. Want to know about *kifaaitkos* (a carrot and pea stew) and *umqombothi* (a traditional beer)? Want to know where to get a famous 'Wembley Whopper' (a spicy hamburger)? This is the stuff of Capetonians as much as Table Mountain and penguins at Boulders Beach.

In a number of chapters, *Cape Town Uncovered* focuses on the historical and historic central city, not because it is the only part of Cape Town of any interest or significance, but because this geographically and demographically eccentric area embodies so much of the complexities of Cape Town today – it is literally where it all happened. Familiar streets and buildings now stand on the place where the destruction of the economy and way of life of indigenous people began 350 years ago, where the first slaves arrived in 1653 and where slavery was abolished 180 years later.

The central city is also where the first racially-based forced removals of African people from District Six took place at the turn of the last century, followed seven decades later by the final destruction of the 60 000-strong inner-city community. It is the location of the South African Parliament – where for over a century, a whites-only legislature solemnly debated and passed colonial and apartheid legislation – as well as the Grand Parade, site of many of the mass struggles and protests against these systems.

Cape Town is a city in transition, a city that is beginning to create a new identity, where cultural diversity is valued, hidden histories and memories recognised, and all citizens feel able to call home. The power of *Cape Town Uncovered* is that, by concentrating on the lives and activities of people and communities, it is able to describe and contribute to a process of transformation in a way that is meaningful to Capetonians and visitors alike.

Andrew Boraine
CHIEF EXECUTIVE: Cape Town Partnership

From cabbage patch *to* neon lights

Once little more than a cabbage patch guarded by a mud-walled fort, Cape Town is now the Mother City of a nation and gateway to a continent. Recently, it has also stepped onto the global stage as one of the world's 10 most popular cities.

Buskers and a 'bergie' combine energies to entertain street crowds during the annual Cape Town Festival.

Concert in the Company's Gardens.

Beachfront at sunset, Sea Point.

Chapter One

From cabbage patch to neon lights

While it is people that give the city soul and sustain its pulse, Cape Town's natural setting is acknowledged as being among the world's most spectacular.

Part of the appeal of Cape Town (population – about three million) is that it is funky, sociable, creative and entertaining, with the sophistication of a world-class city yet also the charm and feel of a small and familiar town. But it could easily never have existed.

In the 17th century, the sea was of paramount importance for the trade upon which empires were built, and strategic ports were therefore essential. The shore of Table Bay was chosen for the site of a settlement, partly because of its sheltered location but also because of the fresh-water streams that cascaded from the mountain down to the sea. It is clear from writings and journal entries at that time that it was never the intention of the Dutch East India Company (commonly known by the Dutch abbreviation VOC – Verenigde Oostindische Compagnie) for the fort at the Cape of Good Hope, begun in 1652, to develop into a town or city. Senior merchant Jan van Riebeeck had strict instructions to establish a refreshment station only and to run the company's business, which included trading with the indigenous peoples who grazed and watered their herds on the slopes of Table Mountain.

However, a permanent settlement became inevitable as 'free burghers', men released from their contracts with the Company, moved from the confines of the fort, were granted land and started farming independently. There was also a need for board and lodging for visitors, who called into the port from all over the world. Van Riebeeck's records show that only four years after the Dutch settled at the Cape, Jannetje van Doesburgh, a sergeant's wife, was allowed to keep an inn outside the walls of the fort. (Incidentally, her licence stipulated that she would 'not be permitted to corrupt the good folk of the fort'!)

Cape Town now reaches from Cape Point to Table Mountain and across the Cape Flats, but mention of its name usually brings to mind the city centre, wedged between the mountain and the waters of Table Bay. The centre of the city roughly matches the area of the 17th-century Dutch settlement, which was known as the 'Caabse Vlek' (meaning 'market town' or 'borough'). It stretched from Buitenkant to Buitengracht streets, and from the foot of the mountain to the original seashore, which was near Strand and Waterkant streets. The streets in the old town were laid out with Dutch precision in an orderly grid, with *grachts* (canals), but this has not stifled their modern character. Today, shops and restaurants spill over onto the pavements, typified by the antique- and flea-market stalls in the pedestrians-only section of Church Street, which sit cheek by jowl with coffee-shop tables where friends or business associates meet.

In contrast to many central business districts (CBDs) around the world, Cape Town's city centre is vibrant and expanding, and is attracting large-scale local and international investment. It has a character that sets it apart from any other city in the country, yet is also firmly rooted in the emerging, multicultural South African identity. Even this is an evolving one, though, richly contributed to by a steady stream of arrivals from its northern neighbouring states. The city's built environment reflects the diverse cultures of the people who, through its history, have made Cape Town their home. Though most of Cape Town's buildings are relatively modern, there are a few examples of 17th- and 18th-century Dutch architecture remaining in the city centre, along with some later Victorian façades. Among the more attractive is the cluster of buildings round the Company's Gardens, which include the Tuynhuys, adjacent to Parliament, and the Iziko South African Museum.

Koopmans de Wet House, Strand Street.

The Castle of Good Hope still stands as a powerful reminder of Cape Town's beginnings. And of the few other buildings that have been preserved almost unchanged since the Dutch period, there are two of particular interest in Strand Street – Martin Melck House (1781), now the Gold of Africa Museum, and Koopmans de Wet House (1791), also a museum. In a tradition starting with Marie Koopmans de Wet, whose grandmother bought the house in 1804, there have always been people with a strong sense of heritage in Cape Town. This probably helped to save many buildings of historical value from being demolished in the 1950s and 60s to make way for the wave of corporate skyscrapers that were built at that time.

While it is people that give the city soul and sustain its pulse, Cape Town's natural setting is acknowledged as being among the world's most spectacular. The city provides an interesting counterpoint to its imposing natural environment. It borders the Table Mountain National Park, which stretches from Signal Hill to Cape Point and contains the treasures of the Cape Floral Kingdom. The city's geography is probably what sustains its heartbeat. The city centre is small and contained. Psychologically, a small city centre with cultural and historical landmarks in close proximity to each other, as well as an active commercial sector, gives people a sense of being at the hub of activity. The presence of the mountain and sea also creates a feeling of being 'somewhere'. Natural features give people a sense of security, a sense of place in the landscape. And few natural features seem as solid and reassuring as Table Mountain, whose iconic status is as powerful as the Empire State Building in New York, Rio de Janeiro's Sugarloaf, London's Big Ben or the Eiffel Tower in Paris.

Business Buzz

For at least 200 years, Cape Town has supported diverse commercial activity – and for most of those years this activity was concentrated in the city centre, corresponding to today's CBD. While it never completely faltered, trade in the city centre took a knock in the 1960s and 70s with the forced removal of 60 000 inner city dwellers, a consequence of the Group Areas Act. In the 1980s and early 90s, the global trend towards decentralisation also had an impact on the city centre. Factories and industries already existed in outlying areas, but office parks sprang up in the suburbs, apparently for greater safety and relief from traffic congestion. However, the CBD has gone the route of others across the world in planning fundamental improvements to woo back people and businesses – the lifeblood of any metropolis.

The success of this plan is evident in the range of people with diverse skills who now base

The leisure culture is helping to define a new, 21st-century identity for the heart of the city.

Top: Saturday afternoon at the V&A Waterfront. Above: Shooting a British feature film, Nyanga.

themselves in the city centre. These young go-getters are setting the trend and the standard by which the city will be run, contributing to the emergence – and attraction – of money-spinning industries, such as film, ICT (information communication technology), fashion and tourism – the fastest-growing industry locally and nationally. With this change has come the 'cappuccino culture' lifestyle – exemplified in the pavement cafés, restaurants and clubs that line Long Street, formerly the domain of small, family-run businesses which offered tailoring and alterations, electrical goods or fish and chips. Indeed, the leisure culture is helping to define a new, 21st-century identity for the heart of the city. People in the advertising field, film and music industries and even ICT use the cafés and coffee shops as their 'office away from the office'. Here, and in a plethora of clubs, they rub shoulders with hip-hop and beat boys, dreadlocked skateboarders, hipster-bellbottomed models, well-gelled bad boys and wannabe MCs and rock stars.

Cape Town's commerce is also driven by the port, which throughout the city's history has been instrumental in maintaining its connection with the outside world. Seated at the foot of Africa, Cape Town would otherwise have been quite isolated. Before air travel became popular, in the late 1960s, the harbour was alive with activity. Mail and passenger ships called, there was a 'penny ferry' service from the old Clock Tower to the former port captain's wharf in the Victoria Basin, people fished off the pier and fishermen brought the day's catch from Granger Bay to a fish market at Roggebaai – where skyscrapers now stand.

In the 1940s, the foreshore was developed, on reclaimed land that extended along Adderley Street, from the railway station precinct to the new shoreline. This extension to Adderley Street (as it was named under British rule) resurrected the street's original name, Heerengracht, which trans-lates as 'the gentlemen's canal'. The motorways that later accompanied the foreshore development sterilised a swathe of land between the centre of town and the harbour. And the new and busy container terminal restricted people's access to the water's edge, breaking a long Capetonian tradition of wandering along the docks, pausing to watch goods being loaded or offloaded from the boats. But sentimentality aside, the industrialisation of the port has played an important part in sustaining Cape Town's commercial success.

Now a new wave of development on the foreshore has included imposing multistorey hotels and the Cape Town International Convention Centre, which are effectively luring people to the heart of the city. Ironically, the Victoria & Alfred (V&A) Waterfront, a development that might have drawn business and interest away from the city centre, has in fact played a significant role in restoring its vibrancy. In the late 1980s, when the CBD was a little unfashionable, developers planned an ambitious, high-risk investment on the waterfront, which was largely a derelict area.

It proved to be a runaway success. Like waterfront developments throughout the world, it has contributed to the revitalisation of the city centre and, through reconnecting people with the water, has revived Cape Town's identity as a harbour city. Today, the Waterfront and the city are linked not just by road but also by the Roggebaai Canal, which is now navigable by water taxi.

Island of Tribulation

The V&A Waterfront area is a thriving commercial venture – entertainment mecca, exclusive residential marina and tourism drawcard. One of its features is the Nelson Mandela Gateway to Robben Island, launchpad for trips to the island which is now a South African National Monument and a World Heritage Site. Before European settlement, the island was used as a refreshment stop for passing ships whose crews believed the Khoekhoen on the mainland were cannibals. The sailors dined on seals and penguin eggs – the latter were regarded as a delicacy well into the 1800s, until the penguin population became extinct. African penguins were reintroduced in the 1980s and now there's a thriving population, along with plenty of other birds and animals, including three species of tortoise.

Robben Island is usually associated with the incarceration of Nelson Mandela, who was on the island as a political prisoner from 1964 to 1982, when he was transferred to the mainland until his release in 1990. With Mandela, who became South Africa's first democratically elected president, were other fathers of the struggle such as Walter Sisulu, Govan Mbeki, Ahmed Kathrada and

Nelson Mandela on a commemorative visit to the limestone quarry on Robben Island where, as a prisoner, he did hard labour.

Tourists in the Robben Island prison courtyard, being shown a photo of former inmates mending old clothes at the same spot.

Robert Sobukwe. They followed a long line of political prisoners isolated on the island, dating back to Autshumato (also known as Harry the Strandloper), who was banished there in 1658 for taking back cattle that his people (the Khoekhoen) believed the Dutch colonists had unfairly confiscated. Incidentally, he was one of the few to escape successfully from the island. Other leaders who were imprisoned on Robben Island included Muslim holy men from the East Indies who resisted Dutch domination and, in 1749, Daing Mangenam, Prince of Macassar. In the 1800s, defiant Xhosa chiefs such as Maqoma and the prophet Makana were also banished there.

In the mid-1800s, Robben Island served as a hospital for the mentally ill, lepers and people with other chronic diseases. One mental patient, known as Plaatjes, would scour the beach for flotsam and build himself a boat, presumably to escape the island. The story goes that hospital staff would keep an eye on him and as soon as he was putting the final touches to the boat, they would burn it. He would watch sadly and then start again, in an unending cycle, until he died.

After a short spell as a military base during the Second World War, Robben Island again became a prison in 1961, entering perhaps its most infamous period in history. Apart from the political and common-law prisoners, a community of warders and their families lived on the island, in the village. The vehicles in which they used to get around are legendary, 'rustbuckets' to say the least – skeleton cars, with entire doors or bonnets missing, their engines miraculously still going. The difficulty of getting vehicles across the 12 kilometres from Table Bay to the island was expensively illustrated in 1997, when a luxury bus being lifted to Robben Island by helicopter plunged into the sea after the cradle that held it broke. The bus was due to transport guests at a fund-raising banquet hosted by President Mandela.

Nelson Mandela, flanked by deputy presidents Thabo Mbeki and FW de Klerk, after Mandela was elected president by Parliament.

Vicky Ntozini and her husband, Piksteel, and baby in their Khayelitsha B&B.

Table Mountain reflected in Molteno Reservoir.

Above: The last sitting of the all-white Parliament in the House of Assembly, prior to the 1994 elections. Below: Weeks later, these benches were filled with anti-apartheid artworks destined to replace the apartheid art in the hallways of Parliament.

Contrasts *make a city's* character

Cape Town is whatever you experience it to be –
at any given moment, in any given place. Its
character is as rich and varied as its history, and
as the diverse people who give the city soul.

Sighting the new moon signalling the end of Ramadaan, Sea Point.

Chapter 2
Contrasts make a city's character

Once a year at sunset, on Sea Point's beachfront, the Muslim faithful scan the sky for the crescent of light that signals the rising of the new moon and the end of the annual month-long fast of Ramadaan – a time for celebration. The sighting of the new moon is a tradition that has been part of life at the Cape since the first Muslims arrived here more than three centuries ago.

In another part of the city, but light years away in cultural terms, 'gay' and 'straight' revellers in fancy dress celebrate something entirely different – among other things, the sexual freedom of the 21st century. The annual MCQP (Mother City Queer Projects) Costume Party is a flamboyantly festive event that is helping to put Cape Town on the international 'pink city' itinerary.

Though the two events rarely coincide, their intersection in December 2001 aptly illustrated the contrasts so characteristic of the city. To accommodate these divergent activities, the city's streets and public spaces are constantly changing, chameleon-like in their adaptability.

The narrow streets of the city centre are often clogged with processions of film and technical support trucks, crews and lighting, reflecting Cape Town's status as one of the darlings of the film industry. And models doing fashion shoots frolic in the Heerengracht fountains or brave the slopes between Rhodes Memorial and the De Waal Drive highway, where wildebeest and zebras usually graze.

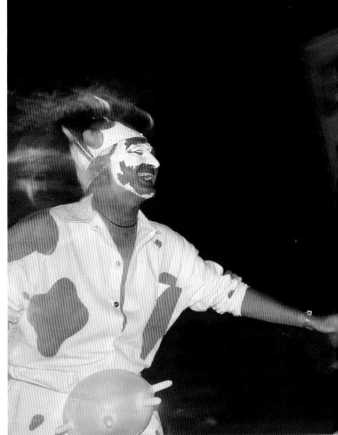

On January 2 every year, Adderley Street – historic artery of the city centre – is awash with a rainbow of flashy-bright satin, music, singing, dancing and crowds of onlookers, as troupes of minstrels parade down part of it in the Cape Minstrel Carnival. At night, during the December holiday season, the street is lit up with a fantastic display of Christmas lights, and shoppers browse among the stalls of a souk-like market. By day, it returns to a noisy, fume-choked, traffic-clogged conduit.

The Company's Gardens, at the top of Adderley Street, have also had many incarnations. Initially the VOC's vegetable patch to supply passing ships with fresh produce, it is now a decorative garden and tranquil spot where those with time on their hands can walk, sit and relax. Art exhibitions are sometimes held in the avenue, competing with the squirrels for attention. And occasionally a concert transforms the quiet lawns into a loud and crowded meeting-place for the many cultures and people that contribute to Cape Town's character.

The Castle, too, hosts a variety of activities. It is still an army barracks, but in addition is a strong tourist attraction, venue for an annual military tattoo, gallery for photo and art exhibitions, and an occasional venue for diplomatic functions. It is also the home of the William Fehr Art Collection and a military museum.

Space to enjoy a quiet stroll, an intense game of chess or a social 'cuppa', the Company's Gardens.

Public spaces, and the festivals and activities that enliven them, are a powerful vehicle not only for building a sense of community in and ownership of the spaces, but also for creating a city's individual person-ality and international profile.

Shooting movies in the city centre.

Common Ground

Busker, V&A Waterfront.

Public spaces, and the festivals and activities that enliven them, are a powerful vehicle not only for building a sense of community in and ownership of the spaces, but also for creating a city's individual personality and international profile. Cape Town's oldest square, the Grand Parade, for example, is a symbol of the development and changes in the life of the city. During the Dutch era, the square was levelled to make a training ground for soldiers. It was conveniently situated between the original mud fort, built on a site behind today's Post Office, and the new Castle, built between 1666 and 1679. The open square was then known as 'Wapen Plijn'. Apart from being a parade ground, it was used in later years for such events as celebrating the governor's birthday with puppet shows, bull-baiting and other sports and entertainment, and for New Year's celebrations.

But the square also had a sombre side. The public execution spot was located where Buitenkant Street today runs past the square's parking area. The place of execution was later moved to Gallows Hill (hence the name), near the present-day traffic department in Green Point.

Crowds greeting Nelson Mandela immediately after Parliament formally declared him President in 1994; Mandela responds from the balcony of the City Hall, Grand Parade.

In the mid-1700s, the square was divided by a wall. On one side, the soldiers trained and on the other, farmers could outspan their oxen and sell their produce. With the second British occupation of the Cape (from 1806), Wapen Plijn was renamed the Grand Parade. It became the centre of social and business activities – especially after the Commercial Exchange, headquarters of the first Chamber of Commerce, was built on the edge of the Parade in 1822. The building was demolished 70 years later. During the 1800s, the Parade was a popular auction site, a tradition that continued for more than a century, before flea-market stalls took over.

Being at the heart of so much activity, the square was also a fashionable meeting-place, where the ladies of the Cape could 'parade' and display their finery, though they were a little put out when prostitutes began to do likewise. In general, though, it was a popular place for family promenades on Sundays, much like the Sea Point beachfront promenade is today.

In more modern times, starting in the 1950s, the Grand Parade was the scene of anti-apartheid protests. And it was the setting for Nelson Mandela's first public speech after he was released from prison on February 11, 1990. He spoke from the balcony of the City Hall to a jubilant crowd that spilled across the tarmac below. By night the square loses its vivacious character, and serves as a parking area for people attending concerts at the City Hall or, occasionally, events at the Castle.

Bread and Butter

Adderley Street from the Heerengracht fountain, Foreshore.

Being adjacent to a large bus terminus and the station concourse, the Parade is a natural focus for commuters from the Cape Flats townships. The city draws in people from every corner, to work in the high-rise tinted-glass buildings of the corporate world or, informally, as entrepreneurs of every imaginable description. People's economic circumstances vary almost as much as the commercial activities they engage in to make a living. At the top end of the scale, the corporate sector is dominated by the oil and financial industries, which occupy the foreshore skyscrapers or office parks in the suburbs. In the middle of the scale is a vast landscape of business space dedicated to retail – from luxury goods to groceries and a fair variety in between. A glance at the glass façades of company headquarters and ornately decorated retail-store windows often interestingly reflects their antithesis – informal vendors positioned on the pavement outside, trying to make a living from selling sweets, cigarettes or cheap sunglasses and, increasingly, tourist knick-knacks.

Some entrepreneurs, like the characterful flower-sellers of Adderley Street, have been a feature of Cape Town for more than a century, and have become synonymous with the city. Others include the more recent flea-market stall-holders at the station, along St George's Mall and in Greenmarket Square, where there is a growing presence of goods and curios from other African countries.

The flower-sellers of Adderley Street ... always ready for a witty exchange.

*CMT ('cut, make and trim'), a traditional Cape Town
industry under threat, Salt River clothing factory.*

Cyber café, Sea Point.

Informal street vendors are a well-established part of the parallel township economy and have an essential role in making goods (especially foodstuffs) available in residential areas – particularly in shantytowns – where no major supermarkets have been established. Unlike in the city centre, their activities in the townships include street-side kitchens, barbecues, hair salons or barber's shops and service centres offering local and international calls, fax and computer facilities (despite the popularity of cellphones). Furniture sales and all manner of mechanical and car exhaust repairs are also common. In addition to fruit and vegetable hawkers, there are meat stalls selling any cut imaginable – including 'smileys' (sheep's heads), a township speciality.

In the city, traditional industries are having to make room for some newcomers fast making an impact. Of the new-generation industries, ICT is the cheeky new kid on the block. With high-level ICT skills, business suss and a good dose of innovation, Cape Town's 'techies' are not only carving out a global niche but have also firmly established themselves as part of the city's business beat – notably in an incubator-style set-up with the requisite high-bandwidth telecommunications infrastructure, appropriately called 'Bandwidth Barn'.

Among the older industries is the rag trade, and clothing factory workers form an essential part of the fabric of Cape Town's trade and industry. Most factories are concentrated in the suburb of Salt River, but once a year the workers discard their overalls and take to the streets of

Fashion show to promote the rag trade, presented by the SA Clothing and Textile Workers' Union at the Whale Well, Iziko South African Museum.

*Entrepreneurial spirit...
Gugulethu; Khayelitsha; and
preparing a 'smiley' sheep's
head, Langa.*

Guest at a B&B, Khayelitsha.

Township tourists playing pool in a shebeen, Khayelitsha.

the city centre, in a gregarious parade that is part of the Spring Festival. The highlight of the event is the crowning of their Spring Queen. For a few hours she is queen of the catwalk, but soon she is back at work behind the scenes, operating a sewing machine and creating off-the-peg garments for trendy chain-stores.

The more glamorous side of the rag trade is, of course, the fashion industry, with no meagre supply of established designers, as well as up-and-coming young talent beginning to make a mark on Cape Town's catwalks. The annual Fashion Week is a magnificent showcase that is now being marketed (among other highlights) to establish Cape Town's appeal as a tourist destination.

Tourism and the hospitality industry are major sources of income, and they generate a significant number of jobs in the city. But it is not only the luxury hotels, abundant guesthouses, B&Bs and backpackers' lodges in the city bowl that are benefiting from the tourism market. Some enterprising township residents have opened up their homes to guests, providing a different perspective of life in Cape Town, with traditional African food and a visit to a shebeen, or beer hall, as part of the experience. There is also a growing number of craft centres and markets in the townships, drawing tourists to the very places where the crafts are made.

Part of Cape Town's challenge is to maintain its contrasts but at the same time to create a flow between the city centre and the fringe, a flow that is based not just on employment, trade and tourism, but also on a sense of ownership – for all Capetonians – of the city.

Taking over the streets during 'Night Vision', part of the Cape Town Festival, city centre.

In festive spirit … Adderley and Wale streets: This page, clockwise from top: Christmas celebrations; watching the Cape Minstrel Carnival; University of Cape Town student 'rag' day; the Gay Pride parade. Opposite: spectators and participants during the Cape Minstrel Carnival.

Company's Gardens.

Cape Town *at* play

The picture of Cape Town at play is as broad and varied as it is complex.

It incorporates sport of almost every description and an imaginative range of

leisure pursuits and hobbies, which people tend to pursue with enormous

passion. That is when they're not simply taking time out to relax …

Winners and losers at the J&B Met, Kenilworth.

Walk, run, skate, sit, cycle.
The Promenade, Sea Point.

Fly, sail, ski, swim, surf. Bloubergstrand.

'The Chains', Lion's Head.

Chapter 3
Cape Town at play

When there's such variety to choose from, personal preference naturally steers people in particular directions, but environmental and economic circumstances also dictate how they spend their leisure time. For those to whom the mountain and sea are easily accessible, there are outdoor options to suit almost any pocket. But for many people living in impoverished circumstances in any of the Cape Flats townships, outdoor activities more often than not mean playing in the street or on an open patch of ground or a makeshift sportsfield. Indeed, sport and leisure pursuits and facilities still reflect historical and racial divisions, though activities are sometimes purely a reflection of cultural preference. Conversely, sport and leisure are areas that provide plenty of opportunity for social integration.

Sport spans the new adventure trend, international events, team and solo, as well as activities supported by Cape Town's natural environment. For outdoor enthusiasts, the long summer evenings are a bonus, allowing them to run, walk or mountain-bike after work, even during the week. Once you start noticing them, sports fanatics seem to overrun Cape Town. Inevitably, and almost anywhere, there are people jogging or a huddle of cyclists togged out in goggles, crash helmets and tight-fitting lycra. When the wind is just right, paragliders drift lazily down from Lion's Head to land on Camps Bay beach, as if the process were as simple as stepping into an elevator and pressing G for ground. There are people launching themselves from Table Mountain (base jumping or, attached to a rope, abseiling), sandboarding, kiteboarding or kayaking. Almost every extreme adventure sport is on offer, creating a burgeoning industry in the city centre and putting Cape Town on the international map of the adrenaline junkie. This, as well as the growing coffee-shop culture that fills the sidewalks, is shaping a stimulating, young-at-heart personality for the city centre, the oldest part of Cape Town.

Some sport and leisure experiences, such as the Cape-to-Rio Yacht Race and the Volvo Ocean Challenge, are centred on the harbour. Others link the heart of the city, via its arteries, to the periphery, such as the internationally known Old Mutual Two Oceans Marathon and the Pick 'n Pay/Argus Cycle Tour. Whether the runners and cyclists draw on the stunning scenery as a motivation or see it only as a sweaty blur, the scenic routes are a drawcard for these events. It is this interplay between the heart of the city and the urban sprawl that gives Cape Town such a colourful personality, with activities to match. People are regularly out walking, hiking or rock climbing – along a maze of pathways horizontal and vertical – from Table Mountain to the tip of

Cape Point, throughout the Table Mountain National Park. To add to the existing trails, a new route, the Hoerikwaggo Trail (the Khoekhoe name for Table Mountain, translated as 'sea mountain'), is being prepared and will stretch between Table Mountain and Cape Point, with five or six overnight stops.

The less physically inclined may choose to use the cable car to conquer the mountain or simply appreciate it from a distance. But tourists and locals are increasingly opting for a more intimate experience of nature, with the added dimension of the Cape Floral Kingdom's fynbos vegetation. The mountain was one place where apartheid never applied, and people of all backgrounds and from all residential areas have always enjoyed its hikes and pathways.

Left: Fans of the city's mascot football team, Ajax Cape Town, Newlands Stadium.

Above: Street soccer, Khayelitsha.

The Sporting Scene

The tote has long been popular across the racial and social spectrum, and flashy horseracing events, such as the annual J&B Met at Kenilworth Racecourse, have relatively recently become a multicultural show of extravagant fashion that draws as much attention as the rippling horse-flesh.

Soccer has traditionally been more popular in the townships. But its fan base is broadening and, though matches are still played in Athlone or Green Point, the formerly white-dominated rugby ground at Newlands Stadium is now the home of Ajax Cape Town, the local arm of the Dutch international soccer giant. Matches held there compete with rugby and cricket in drawing capacity crowds. In its heyday, the Seven Stars club – representing Cape Town's seven townships – was a springboard for soccer stardom, launching football wizards such as Quinton Fortune, who went on to play for Manchester United, and Benni McCarthy, who became a star striker with FC Porto. Seven Stars was swallowed up with the formation of Ajax Cape Town, which, with Santos and Hellenic, are the main Cape Town clubs – though some township soccer aficionados more passionately support either of the Johannesburg arch-rivals, Kaizer Chiefs and Orlando Pirates.

Above: 1989, the Strand.

Right: First Beach, Clifton.

Above: First Beach, Clifton. Below: Beach photographer plying his trade, Muizenberg.

Competition, health or friendship – cycling's the common thread. The Cape Argus Cycle Tour, gym, or a social cycle along the Sea Point Promenade.

A startling experience for some – swimming with penguins, Boulders Beach, Simon's Town.

Fishing fever takes over, Hout Bay.

An intriguing aspect of township sports fans is that their sporting preference often reflects their origin. Ndabeni, for example, had the first township cricket club, apparently because most of the people living there came from the Eastern Cape, where cricket had been popular since British colonial times. Age also plays a role. The older men are fond of rugby, seeing it as a 'real man's' game, whereas basketball has a huge following among township schoolkids. Boxing is ever-popular, especially in Khayelitsha and Langa, and there's a growing interest in golf (already the pastime of choice for many affluent Capetonians and businesspeople of all races). Volleyball is a relative newcomer to the townships, but it is beginning to catch on.

Venturing into the water, there is much to be experienced beneath the waves as well as on the surface. Scuba-diving is one of the fastest-growing sports in Cape Town. Farther out to sea, underwater adrenaline junkies can come face-to-face with Great White sharks. In an interesting role-reversal, humans do their watching from behind bars inside a metal cage.

Surfers occasionally have brutal encounters with sharks, but it generally doesn't seem to keep them out of the water for long. Neither sharks nor the icy Atlantic waters ruffle the cool of the wet-suit-clad surfers, whose sub-culture enriches the multilayered life of Cape Town. Other lovers of water sports include windsurfers, sailing enthusiasts and deep-sea fishermen, who return home with a catch worthy of repeated tall stories. Their land-bound cousins stay firmly rooted to the rocks or sand as they cast their lines out for the catch.

For the more laid-back, who think beaches are purely for relaxation, there's plenty of room to laze on the sand, drink sundowners with friends, enjoy a family picnic, take a leisurely walk or cool off in the water. Though beaches are multicultural and non-racial, there are still certain spots frequented by particular groups of people – especially on New Year's Day. And there is a sort of insiders' code to the different categories – surfers' hangout, children and dogs, good swimming, romantic strolls or trendy place to be seen.

A beachfront wall becomes backdrop to playful vignettes, Camps Bay.

Clockwise from top: Clifton, Strandfontein,
Bloubergstrand.

New Year's Day, Sandvlei, Muizenberg.

Skiing on artificial snow and paragliding within metres of each other on the same day, Bloubergstrand.

Picnickers, Lion's Head.

A netball game, Gugulethu.

Playing dominoes, Khayelitsha.

Township cinema, Philippi.

Out to Play

At night, clubbing, which includes a variety of gay venues, has become de rigueur in all parts of the city, matched in the townships by clubs and shebeens. At the heart of them all are drinking, music and dancing. The sex industry also comes alive after dark. In Cape Town it is traditionally centred on Sea Point Main Road, but also operates in the suburbs and townships. The adult entertainment industry in general is becoming increasingly overt, with columns-worth of 'smalls' advertisements in the local press and a rash of adult-entertainment shops appearing on city streets.

The city has an extraordinary number of restaurants, and eating out is a major leisure activity – any night of the week. Some of the most popular venues offer live music, provided by a variety of local bands. But aside from restaurants, Cape Town has gigs covering almost any style of music – from folk to funk, R&B, rock and rap, jazz and kwaito. And if listening to music is not enough, amateurs can join traditional African djembe drum circles to connect with their internal beat.

The annual Gay Pride parade, Green Point.

The premier jazz event on Cape Town's calendar is the annual North Sea Jazz Festival, now renamed the Cape Town International Jazz Festival, which features local and international artists. The increasing number of international artists and groups visiting to perform here gives local bands a much-needed opportunity to play to a wider audience and gain valuable exposure as 'warm-up' acts. There is also the four-day, 80-hour Jazzathon – with its special focus on local and emerging musicians – which has become a staple for music lovers. It too is held annually, at the V&A Waterfront Amphitheatre. All year round, Manenberg's Jazz Café and the Green Dolphin at the Waterfront are a melting pot of Capetonian jazz-lovers and tourists from all over the globe.

In the townships, music is the core of leisure time – whether it comes from a radio, 'ghetto blaster' or live band. For a somewhat different musical experience – to be enjoyed on long summer evenings – Sunday concerts at Kirstenbosch National Botanical Garden, along the eastern flank of Table Mountain, are an opportunity for people to relax and have a picnic on the lawn before sitting back to enjoy the music.

Start of the Cape-to-Rio Yacht Race, Table Bay.

Punters and fashionistas at the J&B Met, Kenilworth.

Singer Sibongile Khumalo, legendary trumpeter Hugh Masekela and guitarist Jimmy Dludlu at the North Sea Jazz Festival, 2003, Cape Town.

The fans... Above: Concert of SA export band Just Jinger, Bellville; Below: North Sea Jazz Festival, 2004.

Summer Sunset Concerts, Kirstenbosch Botanical Garden.

Above: Community theatre workshop, Gugulethu.

Below: 'New Day', a production marking 10 years of democracy in South Africa; Fikile Mvinjelwa in 'Aida', Artscape theatre.

Anything Goes

When it comes to leisure pursuits, there is nothing too unusual or obscure to have a following. Any evening of the week, there are people attending pottery, painting, drawing, quilt-making and a number of other arts and crafts clubs and classes. There are creative-writing guilds, poetry-reading groups and book clubs galore, numerous societies – astronomical, archaeological, historical and the like – as well as 'friends of' all manner of interest groups, including the Iziko South African Museum, the Rondebosch Common, Liesbeek River and Mostert's Mill. Chess games are played alfresco in the Company's Gardens and fanatics can play at the Green Point club almost 24 hours a day. Chess is also popular among township residents, who sometimes play on street corners or outside shebeens. But pool is the current trend – whether it is played by adults in a shebeen, between sips of beer, or by children in a yard, on a makeshift table. Dominoes is almost as popular and is usually played with great flourish on a table or platform set up outside, in a back yard or recreational area. And mrabaraba, a board game that can also be played in the sand, is a favourite among children.

Though games still have a place in township leisure time, videos and television dominate. Local residents often congregate on a Saturday afternoon at a shebeen or someone's house to watch televised sports matches, while in the city and suburbs, pubs with big-screen televisions draw the crowds. At shopping malls across the city, movies are essential entertainment and, though there are no cinemas with plush seats in the townships, a converted shack is good enough to provide some movie magic by video.

*Clockwise from left: Scenes from 'Aida'
and 'Carmen' at Artscape; Athol Fugard
directing 'Sorrows and Rejoicings' at the
Baxter Theatre, Rondebosch.*

Entertainment would not be complete without the theatre. At least 10 amateur dramatic societies are active in Cape Town, some of which have been running for 50 years. They regularly stage musicals and insiders report that there is a serious quest for excellence, spurred on by competition for the coveted Cape Times Awards, Cape Town amateur dramatics' own Academy Awards. Tuesdays and Thursdays are Theatre Sports nights at Artscape – with improvisational TV-comedy-style fun. Artscape, on the foreshore, is the centre of the performing arts in the heart of the city. Though its inclusivity today reflects the current focus of South Africa, it was not always so. Formerly called the Nico Malan Theatre, it was a bastion of racial division (and white privilege) during the apartheid era. No mixed audiences were allowed, though as a concession, specific evenings were allocated to coloured audiences.

Defying these racial restrictions was The Space theatre, established in Pepper Street and later transferred to Long Street. It was inaugurated as a club to overcome petty apartheid legislation, which did not outlaw racial mixing in clubs. The brainchild of anti-apartheid playwright Athol Fugard, The Space made it possible not only for all people to be entertained together, but for actors and artists of different races to work and perform together too. The theatre eventually closed its doors in 1979, under political and financial pressure, but it was the project that launched the groundbreaking Market Theatre in Johannesburg.

Now, as South Africa enters the second decade of freedom from apartheid, music and the performing arts, as well as leisure and social activities, continue to foster the process of racial integration in Cape Town.

A scene from 'New Day', Artscape.

Chakras *and* Chickpeas, Sangomas *and* Soothsayers

Go walking on Table Mountain, and somewhere, in a quiet grotto or under a tree, there will be someone meditating – whether simply absorbing and appreciating the beauty and stillness, communing with nature or performing a spiritual ritual.

Greeting the morning mountain from the top of Lion's Head.

Chapter 4

Chakras and Chickpeas, Sangomas and Soothsayers

Many people believe Table Mountain is one of the major energy centres of the world, areas which are said to enhance healing and heighten personal awareness. Whether this has something to do with it or whether it is simply a case of 'supply and demand', Cape Town is truly a centre for spiritual alternatives.

There are scores of complementary health practitioners and African traditional healers, clairvoyants, psychics, astrologers, Feng Shui practitioners, people practising activities often classified as 'New Age', and a proliferation of health and organic food shops, all catering for an even greater number of people who choose these options to support their health and wellbeing.

The annual Art of Living Festival, held in the city, brings together a vast spectrum of esoterica – from colour therapy to crystals. Apart from stalls, mini-sessions and readings, the festival has a full programme of lectures on diverse subjects – from organic foods to Sahaja Yoga and everything in between – all with the common theme of feeding the soul. More regularly, a monthly holistic lifestyle fair in Observatory mirrors the festival, but on a smaller scale.

A major boost to the city's profile on the international spiritual calendar came in 1999, when Cape Town was chosen for the convention of the Parliament of the World's Religions. No less than 4 000 delegates representing most of the world's religions attended the event, which was launched with a procession from the Company's Gardens to District Six. The march was joined by hundreds of participants dressed in traditional cultural and religious attire. Many former residents of District Six – the mixed-race community of 60 000 that was forcibly removed by apartheid legislation in the 1960s – participated in the parliament's ceremonies. It commemorated not only the dispossessed around the world but also the triumph of the human spirit.

The diverse religions and spiritual beliefs represented at the event in some way reflected the spiritual diversity of Cape Town's residents. And although there are some beliefs that are characteristically (but not strictly) linked to certain cultures, most have a cross-cultural following.

A sign language expert translating at a reconciliation ceremony, Company's Gardens.

New Age protesters at the site of a controversial hotel development, Oudekraal.

I Believe, You Believe …

In Cape Town, Islam is closely associated with the Malay community. Their mosques are part of the city's landscape, as is the sight of Muslims wearing long robes and wending their way, as if in meditation, up the steeply inclined streets of the Bo-Kaap, the oldest Muslim section of the city. One of the most important events for Muslims is Ramadaan, the month of fasting. It is the ninth month of the lunar calendar and the month in which the Qur'an was revealed to the holy Prophet Muhammad. Muslims start their fast at sunrise and end it at sunset every day. At the end of the lunar cycle, as soon as the sighting of the new moon is officially confirmed, the fast is ended and Eid celebrations begin. Many Muslims celebrate Eid with family, but hundreds also take part in Nakhlistan which, literally translated from Arabic, means a date-palm garden or oasis. It is also the name taken on by the Nakhlistan Feeding Scheme, run from Rylands Estate, Athlone. The scheme is an operation handled with military-style efficiency, in which food is cooked in giant pots over open fires to be distributed to thousands of Cape Town's poor.

For white and coloured members of the Afrikaner Dutch Reformed Church, the Groote Kerk ('big church') in Adderley Street is the symbol of the oldest Christian congregation in South Africa. It celebrates its 300th anniversary in 2005. The original church building was inaugurated

by the Reverend Petrus Kalden on January 6, 1704, in a ceremony attended by the Dutch governor of the Cape. Although the original structure was replaced in 1841 by the present building, the free-standing clock tower is original. A short walk from the Groote Kerk is St George's Cathedral, theatre of High Church liturgy and meeting-place of mainstream Anglicans of multicultural backgrounds. The cathedral is a strong symbol of anti-apartheid resistance, where many rallies in protest against the government of the day were held.

Sangoma (traditional healer) initiation ceremony, Khayelitsha.

   In addition to the traditional Christian denominations, often housed in historical stone churches or cathedrals, there are fundamentalist Christian groups that attract thousands, young and old. They're often at odds with the New Agers – especially when it comes to rituals perceived to be pagan – such as the planting of a peace pole on Table Mountain by representatives of various world religions even before the 1999 Parliament of the World's Religions. Another peace pole was erected during that event – this time on Robben Island. A procession of international religious and spiritual leaders and practitioners bearing the 188 brightly coloured flags of the nations of the world blessed the pole, which bore the words 'May Peace Prevail on Earth'. It is one of 200 000 peace poles worldwide.

   The small but influential Jewish community in Cape Town includes a range of adherents – some orthodox, some progressive and some for whom being Jewish is more a cultural and

ancestral identity than a religious or spiritual one. Cape Town's Jewish population can, by and large, trace its origins back to Lithuanian immigrants who arrived between the end of the 19th century and the 1930s. For this closely knit community, the Great Synagogue in the Gardens has been a revered institution for well over 100 years. More recently, the Cape Town Holocaust Centre and the South African Jewish Museum have been built adjacent to the Synagogue. As important memorial and cultural exhibition venues, they receive visitors, particularly Jews, from all over the world.

In another example of a strong connection between cultural background and religion, Cape Town's Indian community is mostly Hindu – though there are many who follow Islam or other religions. As with Muslim celebrations, such as Eid, Hindu religious festivals bring the Indian community together – sometimes in an effusive public expression of their faith. One such festival is Kavady, a festival originating in the south of India and held between February and May (depending on the corresponding period on the lunar calendar). The festival honours the

Left: At Eid, the Nakhlistan Feeding Scheme's nightlong preparation of food for distribution among the poor, Rylands Estate.

Below: Celebrating Eid, Bo-Kaap.

Celebration... At the Great Synagogue, Gardens; at the Hare Krishna temple, Rondebosch.

healing powers of the deity Lord Murugan, and involves devotees pulling a chariot (the kavady) with hooks embedded in their backs. The better-known Divali festival of lights (traditionally held in India in October and November to celebrate the end of the monsoon) is usually a family event.

A number of other religions of Eastern origin are represented in Cape Town. Most of the devotees, however, do not have a cultural connection. There is a strong Buddhist following, for example, and devotees of the Hindu deity Krishna, commonly referred to as 'Hare Krishnas', have an ashram near Rondebosch station. Distinctive in their saffron robes, they do the rounds in small groups on Rondebosch Main Road or in Greenmarket Square, chanting to the accompaniment of drums and tambourines.

An increasingly common sight is that of Rastafarians with their signature red, yellow and green objects or items of clothing, prompting at least an 'irie' or 'one love' greeting from their fellows. They have established religious communes on the Cape Flats, at places such as Philippi. Some of them specialise in the cultivation, harvesting and application of indigenous roots, bulbs and herbs for medicinal as well as spiritual use. Greenmarket Square, Castle Street and the pavements of Claremont Main Road are some of the places where their roots and herbs are available for sale.

Religion and spirituality are fundamental to the eclectic mix that adds depth and texture to Cape Town's character.

An African Tradition

In the townships, African traditional healers, or *sangomas,* are plentiful and in great demand – for their herbal remedies and for spiritual guidance via their ancestors. Sometimes people suffering an ailment consult only a *sangoma*, whereas others combine this with a visit to a clinic. Though most *sangomas* are African, there is an increasing number of white people who feel they have the calling and embark on training. Consulting a traditional healer is not common among whites, but there certainly are some who call on a *sangoma* for 'space clearing' – perhaps of a new home – to ensure there is no negative energy or presence of 'evil spirits'.

Many township Africans practise their traditional religion, or aspects of it. Despite this fact, when African religion is mentioned in discussions about the introduction of multifaith religious education at school, it is not normally referred to as a religion in its own right. Most commonly, African religion is combined with Christianity, but with traditional religious customs still being observed. These customs include birth rituals, rituals for the deceased, invocation of the ancestors and other ceremonies involving animal sacrifice.

Church services in townships often incorporate African cultural influences and are usually all-day events, in which people clap and dance in ecstatic worship under makeshift marquees. On some Sundays, there is the dramatic sight of groups of people dressed in flowing white robes, performing baptisms in the waters of Zeekoevlei on the Cape Flats or at the beaches on the False Bay coast.

To what extent religion and spirituality have a significant impact on people's collective state of mind, on their awareness and consciousness, is a matter for debate. But what is certain is that they are an integral part of people's identity, that they dictate how people express themselves in public and community life, and they are fundamental to the eclectic mix that adds depth and texture to Cape Town's character.

Sangoma, Gugulethu.

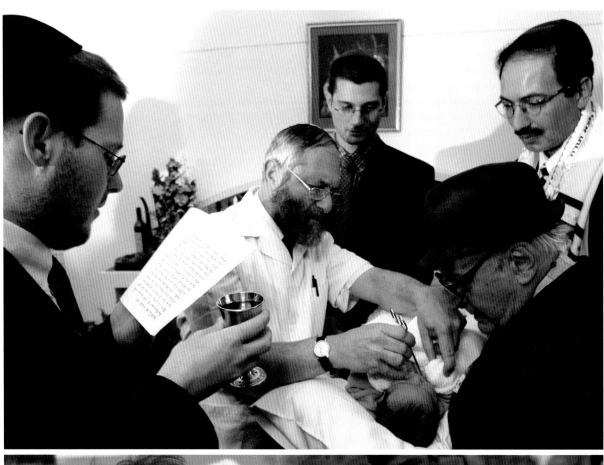

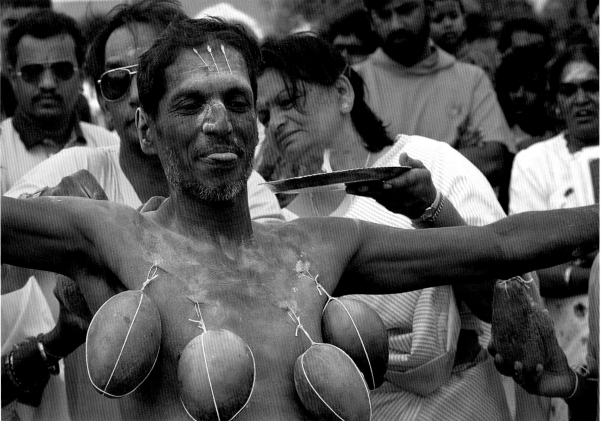

Traditional rituals… Jewish circumcision ceremony; Hindu Kavady festival.

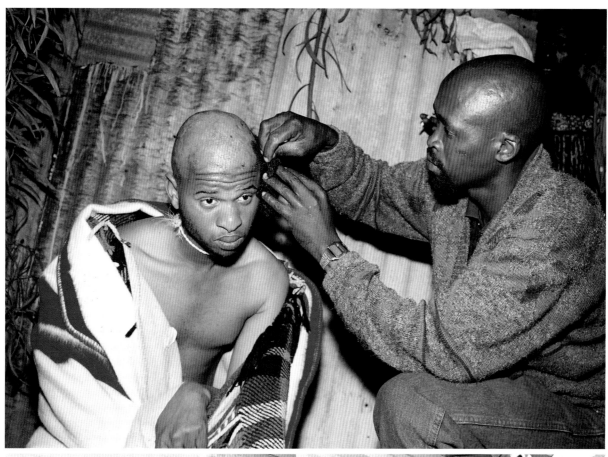

Xhosa initiate Vukile Pokwana at the start of his circumcision, and flanked by fellow initiates afterwards.

In the House of God… (Clockwise from top) Synagogue, Sea Point; Church, Khayelitsha; Hindu temple, Rylands Estate; Mosque, Bo-Kaap.

At prayer... Finding a private moment for prayer. (Right and following page) Prayer rally for Africa, Newlands stadium.

Hare Krishna devotee.

Rastafarian.

St George's Cathedral, city centre.

Hindu temple, Rylands Estate.

Bo-Kaap *and the* 'Cape Malays'

Traditional communities worldwide are under siege. From galloping technology to the pressures of globalisation, they're experiencing a very real threat to the thing they hold most dear – their identity. The Cape

Malaysian community is no exception. Modernity is eating away at the

fabric of its cultural traits and traditional practices. Only time will tell how

long the flame of this former slave community will continue to burn.

Chapter 5
Bo-Kaap and the 'Cape Malays'

The term 'Malay' came to denote a religious rather than an ethnic group, although just the mention of the word conjures visions of colourful dress and intricately woven headgear, spicy and aromatic dishes, elaborate ceremonies and a tradition of song that is vibrantly alive to this day.

Beyond the old city limit of Buitengracht Street, the Bo-Kaap (Upper Cape Town) proclaims itself in a splash of brightly coloured houses. Its steeply sloping cobbled streets define an area that is one of Cape Town's most important historical sites, formerly known as the 'Malay Quarter', and which houses a people of an extraordinary culture and background, who set the Mother City apart from any other city in South Africa.

The Bo-Kaap is the home of a Muslim community once classified as 'Cape Malay', whose roots were established hundreds of years ago by ancestors brought to the Cape as slaves and political exiles, captured by the Dutch on their trade routes during the 17th and 18th centuries – mainly, but not entirely, from what is now Indonesia. The first Malays arrived at the Cape in 1667, but they occupied the Bo-Kaap section of the city only during the 19th century, probably after the emancipation of slaves in 1834.

The predecessors of the present-day occupants of the Bo-Kaap comprised many ethnic groups: Javanese, Arabs, Indians, Sri Lankans, Chinese, Europeans and coloureds, forming a cosmopolitan community constantly undergoing change. Other major influences came from Madagascans, East Africans and Malayo-Indonesians. The fusion of languages, especially Arabic, Malay-Portuguese, Dutch and Malaysian, formed the basis of the creole language that emerged among the slaves and mingled with the language of the Dutch and French Huguenot farming community to eventually evolve into the Afrikaans that is spoken today. Some of the more colourful Malay words to have become part of the mainstream Afrikaans lexicon include *kapok* (cotton wool), *piesang* (banana) and *blatjang* (chutney).

The Malay slaves and exiles brought with them their Islamic culture and faith, and soon Islam was also being embraced by slaves of other origins. The term 'Malay', therefore, came to denote a religious rather than an ethnic group, although just the mention of the word conjures visions of colourful dress and intricately woven headgear, spicy and aromatic dishes, elaborate and intriguing ceremonies and a tradition of song that is vibrantly alive to this day. Under apartheid rule, the community was seen as distinct from those classified as 'coloured' because of its religion and culture.

Among the most celebrated of the political exiles who provided the Cape Malays with their proud history were those from the Dutch East Indies. During the 17th century, with invasions of the Indonesian islands by the VOC under way, local leaders of resistance were exiled to the

Cape. Their artisan skills in cabinet-making and boat- and home-building were highly valued by their Dutch captors. Other slaves, arriving periodically from the East, were put to work on more arduous tasks, including public works projects.

Father of Islam at the Cape

Most important and well known among the exiles who reached these shores was Sheikh Yusuf of Macassar, Indonesia, a remarkable leader of great piety, dignity and culture, who is credited with having established the Muslim Malay community at the Cape. Sheikh Yusuf, brother of the King of Goa, was born in 1626. At the age of 20 he went to Bantam on the island of Java, married the daughter of the Bantamese Sultan and spread the Muslim faith among the local population.

In subsequent years, he stirred intense ire in the VOC, especially in 1683, when he led a protracted uprising of Muslims against the Dutch who were threatening the independence of

Java. He eventually surrendered, under false promises made to him, and was imprisoned for several years before being banished to the Cape by the Dutch, who feared further insurrection by his devout followers. In 1693, Sheikh Yusuf, his two wives, 14 friends and a few servants – a party of 49 altogether – arrived at the Cape aboard the now legendary vessel, the *Voetboog*. Stories of his magical powers abound. One is that when the supply of fresh water failed during the voyage, he dipped his foot in the sea and told his men to let down their casks at the spot. To everyone's amazement, the legend goes, the water was found to be perfectly good to drink. The name 'Voetboog' lives on as the name of a Bo-Kaap street.

Sheikh Yusuf was allowed to live with his group of exiles on the farm Zandvliet, in Faure, for 10 years, continuing to spread his faith among slaves and free persons alike. Simon van der Stel, governor of the Cape at the time, and his son, Willem Adriaan, were among those who befriended and afforded due respect to him. The sheikh died in 1699 and was laid to rest on top of a small sand dune where his *kramat* (holy shrine) overlooks Zandvliet. The site is visited regularly, especially over the four-day long weekend at Easter, in a tradition that has become popular among local Muslims. Sheikh Yusuf's family continued his work until 1704, when arrangements were made to take all but one family member, who had married a local person, back to Macassar. The sheikh's wider circle of converts and followers remained.

Sheikh Yusuf's *kramat* is one of a series that stretches round the Cape Peninsula to form a Circle of Islam which, according to lore, protects the Muslim faithful living within its confines from famine, plague, earthquake and tidal wave. Other *kramats* ritually visited by those preparing for the obligatory pilgrimage to Mecca (the spiritual centre for Muslims the world over) are located in Constantia, on the slopes above Oudekraal beach and the slopes of Devil's Peak, on Robben Island and on Signal Hill.

Bright Colours and Cobblestones

In addition to its social history, the Bo-Kaap has a fascinating architecture. The area includes a number of picturesque cobbled lanes with terraced houses that were probably the homes of European artisans in the 18th or early 19th centuries. The buildings and houses are simple yet charming with their long, low lines, flat-topped roofs and elevated front *stoeps* (verandas), and contrast sharply with the characteristically Arabic domes and minarets of the mosques among them.

Visitors arrive for Eid day lunch, Bo-Kaap.

By the early 1900s, many of the buildings in the Bo-Kaap had started to fall into disrepair. The struggle for their restoration dates from 1943, when a group of Cape Town citizens launched negotiations with the City Council and other authorities for improvements to the area. In 1950, the restoration of one block of 15 houses was completed, but it was only in 1969 that government funds became available for that part of the Bo-Kaap to be proclaimed a historic monument.

Today its continued existence is threatened by increasing gentrification as local and overseas developers and investors realise its international appeal and money-making potential. Pressure is building for established residents to surrender their neighbourhood in return for lucrative offers. Some of the original owners have already started selling up. For the rest of the community, development is an ever-present threat, constantly awake and alert to opportunity.

A Search for Roots Leads East

In 1997, members of the South African Malay Cultural Society became the first local cultural group to visit Indonesia in more than 300 years. They hoped it would be the beginning of greater interaction between the two countries. Two years later, an amazing story that defies all common logic would unfold in that chain of islands.

Ebrahim Manuel, a born-and-bred Capetonian who comes from a long line of fishermen, has always had a sixth sense, a mystic insight he was often tempted to use to bet on horses or playing the Lotto. He was a bit of a drifter who spent most of his adult life travelling the world as a ship's cook, never dreaming that one day he would find a sense of belonging – on a remote island in the Indian Ocean.

His remarkable story begins with a recurring dream in which his father, Toyer, dead for seven years, appeared urging him to explore his family's history. He'd never paid much attention to family ties, but reluctantly started doing some research. He found a family *kitaab*, a book bearing names and inscriptions, in an Arabic script he could not read. He also visited holy sites, such as the mosque in Simon's Town.

'Something strange happened,' says Manuel. 'There's a place where water used to flow down from the *kramat* to the mosque. Since then the site has been developed, so there's no pool there any more, but on that spot I felt an electric shock moving from my feet into my head. I didn't know what it was … and that night I was woken by the same feeling, this time coming from my head down my legs and out my feet. I went to some spiritual people to try to find out

Ebrahim Manuel and detail from a kitaab.

what it was and they said I had a gift passed on from my forefathers … I don't know why – I'm not a spiritual man or a learned man, I'm just a seaman.'

Strange occurrences continued. But, as he started his research, he felt his father's constant presence. 'I didn't even know how to use a computer, but I would be guided to the right place and the right person who could help me every time,' he says.

During this time, he met a visiting Indonesian researcher, Hariyadi Suhada, from the Maritime Museum in Jakarta, who was on a research trip to Cape Town. 'When I took him to the old *koebers* (graveyard) in Simon's Town, where my ancestors are buried, he was surprised to find the inscription on one of the tombstones written in his mother tongue, Buginese,' says Manuel. They found inscriptions on other tombstones in Sanskrit, Melayu and other languages Suhada could understand.

Having gathered enough compelling information, Manuel was strongly convinced that he should make the trip to Indonesia. He went to work as a chef on a boat for about a year to earn enough for his airfare.

'For the first time it really sank in that my family in Simon's Town comes from royalty.'

Once in Jakarta, Suhada and Manuel were unable to find someone to translate Manuel's *kitaab*. So they set off for Sumbawa Island, where Manuel started looking for family links in fishing villages similar to Simon's Town, where he had grown up. They were directed to a village, Pemangong, some distance away in the mountains. After a circuitous bus ride and a long walk into the heart of the jungle, they reached Pemangong and headed for the home of the local imam, Abdul Latief. They were told to wait on the *stoep*.

'Eventually the imam walked towards us. I couldn't believe it – the man coming towards me wearing a sarong and a black fez looked just like my father. He told Hariyadi he knew who I was – "He says you're family of Ismail, who was captured in this village." It was amazing because in my *kitaab* was also the name Ismail.'

Inside his bamboo house, the imam showed them an almost identical *kitaab* also bearing the name Ismail, but with no further information about him or his descendants. He explained that in 1752, Imam Ismail was one of those captured by the VOC, chained and deported for leading resistance against Dutch rule in Pemangong. No one knew where he had gone. Manuel's *kitaab* was the missing link, the secret connection. It picked up from where the other one had left off.

'I am descended from Imam Ismail,' says Manuel. 'The imam told us the old people always used to say that one day Ismail's family would come looking for their relatives. As I hugged and embraced my new family, I could feel the spiritual presence of my father there.'

Manuel, the seventh generation after Ismail, had always believed his family had been slaves of the Dutch. He hadn't even thought about their origin. When Imam Ismail was captured, the Dutch had seized his father, too, Dea Malela, whose name also appears in Manuel's *kitaab*. And Dea Malela, he discovered, was the Sultan of Sumbawa. 'For the first time it really sank in that my family in Simon's Town comes from royalty. My aunt Kobera had always said her mother used to tell her she came from royalty. But we didn't really take it seriously.'

Back in Jakarta, he finally obtained authentic proof of Imam Ismail's ancestry – and ultimately, his own. Knowing that he is descended from Indonesian royalty, and not from slaves, as he had always thought, has had a profound impact on his self-image. Now, with a strong sense of his identity and his roots, and despite the oppression of apartheid and its legacy of forced removal, he has developed true pride in his family's traditions and customs – and their origins in the Indonesian archipelago.

Malaysian cuisine

During the early years of exile in the Cape, it was traditional foods and the rituals surrounding them that can be said to have sustained the Malay community – physically and spiritually.

Malay cooks have always been adept at flavouring the foods that play such a central role in their daily life. A pinch of fragrant allspice or nutmeg would enhance a delicate dish, whereas ground and roasted masala spices were used for more robust dishes, such as breyani (a layered, rice-based dish), denningvleis (a spiced meat stew) or atjar (a pungent condiment made variously from unripe mangoes or diced and sliced mixed vegetables).

The subtle aromas and multilayered undertones of delicately spiced foods present a world all its own – think of *pypkaneel* (stick cinnamon), curry leaves, cardamom, *borrie* (turmeric – known for lending its distinctive yellow colour to curries), ginger, *dhania* (coriander), cloves and nutmeg. Among the better-known Malay dishes that use them are *gheema kerrie* (gheema curry), so called because of the cubed meat it contains, *Penang* curry (of Javanese origin) and a variety of *bredies* (stews) – split-pea *bredie*, sugar bean *bredie*, tomato *bredie*, pumpkin *bredie* and *snyboontjiebredie* (sliced green-bean stew).

Friends, family and passers-by are welcome to participate in Eid day meals, Bo-Kaap.

Particular foods had their particular place on both festive and sombre occasions. *Ingelegdevis* (pickled fish), for example, was a favourite with the not-so-well-off Malay family. It was a common dish especially at long weekends, when the family would pack a picnic basket (which often translated into everything but the kitchen sink) and head for the beach. Much effort – and money – would be spared having a pickled meal ready so that more time could be spent on leisurely pursuits. Alas, the fast-food and take-away culture has largely put paid to this today.

Possibly the most extraordinary of all dishes, however, is the blameless *worreltjies-en-ertjies-bredie* (carrot and pea stew). This dish has a macabre association: it was a favourite served at funerals because it was quick and easy to prepare for the many mourners at the wake. It came to be known – and still is – as *kifaaitkos* (funeral food).

Cape cooking in general has its origins in the dishes brought to the territory by the early European settlers – the Dutch, English and French. But the Malay slave women from the East Indies (particularly from the Batavian, Ceylonese, Javanese and Bengal coasts) are widely regarded as having had the greatest influence on Cape cooking. Their culinary acumen earned them a reputation of excellence as chefs capable of preparing the most inventive and interesting dishes. By all accounts, handsome sums of money were paid for their culinary services.

The Dutch at the Cape often visited Malaysian eateries for their hospitality, spotless premises and reasonably priced menus. The spiced food also satisfied the Dutch yen for exotic dishes, a taste cultivated during their travels to the East. Many years later, the Malay style of cooking would become so infused with the culinary practices of the Dutch that the pure Malay repertoire gradually gave way to a more inclusive one.

And today, with ever-changing food tastes and the growing popularity of dishes from all over the world, Malay food is fast fading into the realm of memory. The genuine article has been so diluted as to have all but disappeared. Even so, there are a couple of restaurants in the Bo-Kaap that serve it, and dishes that hark back to a time of slavery are still cooked in people's homes, though to a diminishing degree: *bobotie* (a baked, spicy, minced meat dish with an egg custard topping), yellow rice and raisins, and *sosaties* (skewered meat) – often enjoyed with *blatjang*.

Taxi *to the* flats

The latest trend to emerge in the wake of post-apartheid

democracy is a frenzied cross-cultural buzz, found not so much

in business or even sports, but rather in the informal taxi trade.

The fares collector.

Chapter 6

Taxi to the Flats

Bontebeuwel.

The road system is positively groaning under the weight and number of these droning shuttles that ferry the masses back and forth

Since the relaxation of regulations that allowed for mass public taxi transport by private operators, there's been an explosion in the number of those easily recognisable Nissan E20 and Toyota Hiace mini-buses, owned mostly by township entrepreneurs. They have become an emblem of black empowerment and self-sufficiency.

The road system is positively groaning under the weight and number of these droning shuttles that ferry the masses back and forth, making sure not only that workers get to their destinations on time, but also that no one is stranded, unable to meet an appointment for leisure or entertainment, even a date …

The real sign that a city such as Cape Town is becoming quite normal in relation to other global destinations is the frequency with which white Capetonians are using mini-bus taxis as a daily means of transport. Today it's become so commonplace, it hardly raises an eyebrow among the usual black and coloured patrons of the taxi routes. But only a few years ago, it was a novelty that highlighted the uncomfortable effects of enforced social segregation.

Consider the scene in the early days, when whites considered taxis 'alternative transport'. The taxi rank on the station deck at the main railway station in Strand Street, just off Adderley Street – the 7.30am Main Road southern suburbs taxi. There's the hip young African dude, sitting next to the young coloured woman, opposite the ever-overalled domestic who's checking out the designer-labelled young white student. On another morning, the snappily dressed, hot bank-teller glances enviously at the couple of white 'beachies', clearly too long-legged for the cramped confines of the mini-bus as they squeeze themselves between two labourers on the back seat.

The edgy white passengers want to be friendly, to engage the poker-faced company, and so laugh out of turn at the first chance – even if it's just a call for fares – or talk incessantly to no one in particular. They find it difficult to interpret the dour early-morning silence – especially in the awkward strain of so many years of enforced cultural separation. Still, they try to establish contact and casual familiarity in a Cape Town minute and at such close quarters …

These days, many white Capetonians use the taxis. Apart from hard-nosed, European inter-national travellers, who've seen it all before and travelled cheek by jowl with the locals in Bangkok, Mumbai and Nairobi, local white taxi travellers have learned the art of blending in. And now their social armoury includes that hundred-yard stare and the no-nonsense bubble-gum chew that serves so well when the conversation has gone 'Afrikaans coloured' or 'township black' and they don't understand a word. Like everything else in Cape Town these days, from going to the beach to democratic national elections, taxi travel, this mini-laboratory of social interaction, has become as normal as every other commercial public interaction in the new South Africa.

Even so, white first-time mini-bus travellers are easily identifiable: always nervous. They've heard some scary stories (not always true) about Cape Town's alternative transportation system and have sworn never to step inside these notorious death-traps. But they're so darned convenient and will drop you exactly where you want to be. That's the attraction. They'll stop anywhere. But they're rarely comfortable. The rule is four to a seat to make up 16 (excluding the driver) before the trip is on – not a fare less. Survival's the name of the game, so 'bums on seats' is the watch phrase. Maximum profit is the aim, even if the gearbox is shot and grinding, the clutch is slipping and the driver is steering with a monkey wrench instead of a steering wheel. 'Work that space,' yells the driver. 'Work it!'

Like everything else in Cape Town these days, from going to the beach to democratic national elections, taxi travel, this mini-laboratory of social interaction, has become as normal as every other commercial public interaction in the new South Africa.

Taxi rank on the central city station deck.

Where the Heart is

Travel from the city centre as far as Mowbray and you have a choice – carry on down Main Road towards the (still) mainly white southern suburbs, or turn left at Durban Road. That'll take you to the Cape Flats with its history of heartbreak and pain, its future lined with an unreasonable sense of optimism and hope. In Belgravia, the Wembley Roadhouse in Belgravia Road is a landmark. Just down the road from Alexander Sinton High School, it was the site of many pitched battles between the security forces of the apartheid era and local youths and neighbourhood activists. This road was the scene of the so-called Trojan Horse incident, when a round of stonings of commercial vehicles erupted one sunny day in October 1985. In the afternoon, railway police hiding inside wooden crates on the back of a government truck suddenly appeared and opened fire. Three young boys were killed, in an outrage that was caught by television camera crews and flighted throughout the world.

Other significant sites of 'struggle' (anti-apartheid resistance) tragedies can be visited by means of several 'township tours', one of which is run by former MK (Umkhonto weSizwe – Spear of the Nation) cadres of the ANC. Some of these tours visit the Langa hostels, which were the terrain of the 1960 anti pass-law demonstrations; Bonteheuwel's Freedom Square, scene of many bloody clashes between police and activists in the 1980s; the Amy Biehl Memorial in Gugulethu, where the young American exchange student was killed by an angry group on September 25, 1993; the spot opposite Athlone Magistrate's Court where two young activists,

Three of the mothers of the Gugulethu Seven: from left, Irene Msinwa, Eunice Miye and Cynthia Ngewu.

Colleen Williams and Robert Waterwich, were killed by a booby-trapped bomb; the house in Athlone where community youth activist Ashley Kriel was shot dead by police on August 9, 1987; and the site of the 1986 Gugulethu Seven Massacre, where unarmed men were fatally ambushed, also by police.

The visits may also include places like the Guga S'thebe arts and crafts project and the Tsoga Environmental Centre, both in Langa, or the homes of *sangomas* in the black townships, where visitors get to taste the traditional African brew called *umqombothi*, made from fermented maize and cornmeal. (More familiar bottled brews can be had at any one of the myriad shebeens, or beer halls.) At another home, in Athlone, visitors may taste traditional Malay dishes, mutton *breyani* (a very spicy rice and meat dish) and chicken curry. For township 'cuisine', a stopover at the Wembley Roadhouse is obligatory. This American-styled 'park 'n eat' is famed for its 'Wembley Whopper', a very authentic burger with a distinctive *masala*-spice flavour. Other specialities are the Gatsby (a giant French loaf stuffed with any of a combination of chips, Vienna sausages or polony), the salomie (chicken, mutton, beef or bean curry wrapped in a *roti*, a pan-fried flatbread), and a double-storey-high toasted *masala* steak sandwich.

The roadhouse is just a minute away from Rylands Estate, home of one of the oldest Indian communities on the Cape Flats, which also contributed significantly and suffered casualties during its support of the freedom struggle. Some members of this community trace their history to the 1860s when their forefathers arrived as indentured labourers in Natal, or to so-called 'passenger Indians' who travelled to Cape Town of their own volition.

Anti-apartheid protests, 1988, Athlone.

The Beat Goes On

The Cape Flats experience is not complete without a visit to one of the nightclubs and an evening of music. Black Americans have their early gospels and spirituals, drawn from the Mississippi Delta area and an ancestry that's rooted in the continent of Africa. On the Cape Flats, when the mood catches you, you can go to the always-thumping Galaxy nightclub in the Westend entertainment complex in Rylands Estate. This is one of the venues where jazz has been adapted to a particular 'township' style by musicians like the legendary saxmen Robbie Jansen, Basil Coetzee, Winston Mankunku Ngozi, McCoy Mrubata and the brothers Duke and Ezra Ngcukana. Added to this fine collection is the returned exile and pioneer musician Abdullah

Ibrahim, famous for the composition *Manenberg – Where It's Happening*. 'Township jazz' has always had a strong local following, mostly among older folk.

At some venues you'll find traditional music, including African marimba, which was once associated with people from rural areas but is undergoing a popular revival prompted by the tourism industry. At the modern-day township disco, however, you'll find a more youthful crowd jiving to a different DJ – modern house, R&B, kwaito, retro-funk, hip-hop and breakbeat music. Brand labels like Fubu, Diesel, Soviet and Tommy Hilfiger are the dress code and passport to a hipness that fuses cultures and melts away differences.

From left: Brothers Duke and Ezra Ngcukana, Robbie Jansen, Abdullah Ibrahim, Freshly Ground and Art Mathews of Just Jinger.

Jam sessions, Gugulethu and Nyanga.

Above: Amampondo, Kirstenbosch Botanical Garden. Below: SA Army Band, Parliament.

CAPE TOWN LINGO

Whether you're in a taxi or walking through the Grand Parade market, chances are you will hear a peculiarly Capetonian lingo. It derives from a mixture of Afrikaans, Cape Flats creole and surf slang, and is spoken with a characteristic sing-song tone.

You'll often hear the words 'Naai, man!' (pronounced 'nigh mun'), which is a variant of the Afrikaans 'Nee man!' and means 'No, man!'. It is also pronounced 'knee mun'.

You'll hear 'entjie' (pronounced 'enchie'), which is slang for 'cigarette'. For example: 'Gee my 'n entjie' ('Give me a cigarette'). Notice there's seldom the politeness of a 'please' or 'thank you'; it's generally regarded as an optional – and often unnecessary – extra. The reply to the ciggie question? 'Naai, man!'

Other 'local is lekker' (local is nice) words include 'chommie' (friend), 'babelaas' (hangover), 'gatvol' (fed-up), 'skollie' (thug), 'pel' or 'pellie' (friend), and 'ek sê!' (an affirmative expletive meaning 'I tell you!').

A 'bergie' is an alcoholic down-and-out who lives on the street, despite the word meaning 'mountain dweller', which referred in the past to outlaws who sought refuge on Table Mountain, and 'bru' means 'brother'.

(These gems have even made their way into the *South African Concise Oxford Dictionary*, dubbed 'the ultimate authority on South African English'.)

Then there are general South Africanisms:

'Jawellnofine' (translated literally as 'yes, well, no, fine' and roughly meaning 'well, okay then', or 'be that as it may' for the more pompous);

'Make a plan' (as in 'we'll make a plan', when simply 'plan' or 'planning' will do);

'Eina' (pronounced 'ay-nah', derived from a Khoekhoe word meaning 'ouch');

'Lekke' (an expression of enjoyment);

'Donner' (pronounced 'dawner', meaning to beat up someone); and a particularly popular one:

'Ag shame!' pronounced like the 'ach' in 'achtung' and not meant as an expression of disgust at all, but rather of pity or, depending on the context, even as a compliment: 'Isn't that sweet hey? Ag shame …'

Cape communities *from* past to

There was a time, not so long ago, when Cape

Town was fragmented by apartheid urban

planning and separate development policies –

a form of social engineering. The cosmopolitan

community that had lived right in the heart of

the city, giving it warmth and soul, was uprooted

and dumped on the barren expanse of the

present-day Cape Flats.

N2 highway, from the city to Cape Town International Airport.

present

Chapter 7

Cape communities - from past to present

The majority of residents of today's coloured and African townships, neighbourhoods and communities can trace the establishment of their present homes directly to the city's dark past, a time that left an indelible mark on the reality – good and bad – that is Cape Town today.

It is perhaps not surprising that for years the CBD struggled to maintain a commercial momentum after the customers who had supported it and lived on its doorstep were removed to areas so distant that it made shopping in the city prohibitively expensive. For them it became difficult to retain any meaningful contact with the city centre. Even now, for a new generation of township residents, the city can be quite alienating, undergoing constant transformation in terms of new buildings, the upgrading of businesses to international standards for tourists, with prices many locals can't afford, and the relatively new phenomenon of refugees from battle-scarred African nations establishing trade in the city centre.

For many, contact with the city usually focuses exclusively on work. And the young people seen enjoying the delights of the city – shopping, romance in the Company's Gardens, a quick bite at one of the many fast-food sit-down eating places – are likely to be there principally because of the proximity of colleges and other educational and training institutions, like the Cape Technikon (now the Cape Peninsula University of Technology) in District Six.

While most African and coloured citizens may have few reasons beyond these to come and enjoy their city, the idea of 'going to town' still lingers – especially among the older generation. This might well be linked to a subconscious connection to a time when 'town' was closer to 'home'.

The result of this physical disconnection was the development, by default and for reasons of survival, of an intra-township economy, a lively industry of small businesses, spaza shops, other informal trade and dogged entrepreneurship.

District Six homecoming ceremony marking the return of former residents.

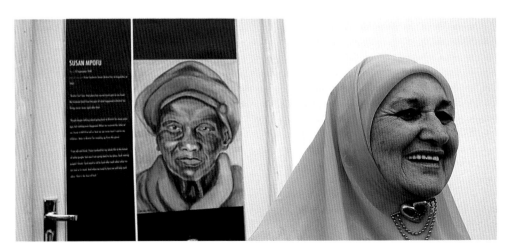

A History of Exclusion

The removal of communities from Tramway Road, District Six and other areas to the Cape Flats wilderness established the bizarre South African phenomenon of 'inside-out' cities.

Urban planning at the Cape dates back to 1653, the year after the Dutch set up their refreshment station, when the VOC declared that private residences were to be built no closer than 200 yards west of the original fort. The forced physical exclusion of certain groups of people began when the Dutch effectively robbed the local nomadic Khoekhoen of part of their grazing land and limited their freedom of movement. Centuries later, in 1901, there was an outbreak of bubonic plague, carried to the Cape aboard merchant ships from the Far East. The disease was associated with poverty and the poor conditions under which black Africans, many of whom worked at the docks, were living in the city. So the city fathers used it as a pretext to move about 5 000 people to a state farm called Uitvlug, later known as Ndabeni, Cape Town's first black 'location'. (Ironically, *uitvlug* translates as 'excuse, pretext or subterfuge'.)

Little more than a decade later, in 1918, when the Spanish flu epidemic hit Cape Town, black Africans were again identified as a health risk. But this time Ndabeni was viewed as being too close to 'white' Cape Town, and the 'undesirables' were forcibly removed to Langa, separated from the rest of the city by roads and railway lines.

Increasing industrialisation over the next 30 years resulted in an influx of job-seeking Africans, particularly from the Eastern Cape, and townships such as Gugulethu and Nyanga sprang up on the Cape Flats. With the Group Areas Act of 1950, separation based on racial grounds became official apartheid policy.

The removal of communities from Tramway Road, District Six and other areas to the Cape Flats wilderness established the bizarre South African phenomenon of 'inside-out' cities. The poor (the 'non-whites') were removed from the inner cities and resettled out on the fringe, not only away from the exclusively white city, but also far from jobs and economic opportunities.

The first government eviction notices were served in 1957 on residents of places such as Three Anchor Bay, Sea Point, Clifton, Camps Bay and Bakoven on the Atlantic seaboard, Tamboerskloof, Oranjezicht and parts of Gardens in the City Bowl, Newlands in the southern suburbs, and Simon's Town. Residents were given a period of two years in which to vacate their homes and were forced to move to areas such as Duinefontein, Maitland, Woodstock, Steenberg, Salt River, Walmer Estate, Athlone and Ocean View.

From far left: Former residents plan their return to Tramway Road, Sea Point; the scar of the Tramway Road community, Sea Point; District Six homecoming ceremony.

The plight of one such community, that of District Six, has been well documented internationally. Sixty thousand residents were forcibly removed from District Six between 1968 and 1981. Today, nearly 40 years after being declared a whites-only area, the first groups of families from among the 2500 ex-residents who submitted land restitution claims have taken ownership of new homes. The process continues.

Homecoming

For other, less-publicised communities afflicted by the Group Areas Act, the dream of a genuine homecoming is also starting to come true. One such community is formerly of Sea Point's Tramway Road, led by their determined campaigner Leonard Lopes. For the 42 families of Tramway Road, their nightmare started in 1959 when they received the government eviction notices cynically referred to as the 'love letter'. They were moved out, and their houses were flattened and replaced by a municipal park which cut Tramway Road in two. The top half was renamed Ilford Road.

As a child, former resident Elizabeth Mitchell had an integral connection with Cape Town. The oldest of seven children, she remembered going to the Moravian school in District Six as a seven-year-old. Her face lit up as she recalled in an interview what she fondly referred to as 'the good times'. She told her story with a disarming cheerfulness that belied the upheaval she and the rest of her community had to endure.

'My mother taught us to manage on our own. She said there's other kids to be seen to and nobody can cart me around. So every morning I took the bus at the bottom [in Regent Road, Sea Point] to go to school. I paid two pennies from here to Cape Town and one penny from Cape Town up Hanover Street to school.

'In the afternoon I would eat sweets that I bought – a whole handful of sweets, six for a penny.' The memory jogged a chuckle from her. 'And if we were very hungry, my schoolfriends and I would walk down to Muir Street in District Six where there was a banana stall. Then I'd walk down to St George's Street to get my bus home. I couldn't walk home to Sea Point – what time would I get there? My mother would be mad!'

On Monday or Tuesday afternoons she would stop off along the route to collect laundry for her mom to do, 'and when I was big enough, about 12, I used to help her with the washing and the ironing'. After Mitchell left school in Standard 6, she worked as a 'charlady' at the nearby

Marlborough Mansions and, later, as a housemaid/waitress at the nearby Kingsbury Hotel.

One inconvenience of living in Tramway Road was that the toilet was in the backyard. But although there was a bathroom in the Bonteheuwel home Mitchell and her family were moved to, 'the life in Sea Point was much better because the community was very close-knit'.

The first Christmas after the evictions was, she said, 'very sad for me because we lived in the desert at No 3 Kersboom Street in Bonteheuwel. That Christmas morning the wind blew so much, we couldn't open the door because all the sand blew into the kitchen. We had sand all over our food.'

Mitchell's mother-in-law died suddenly, just five months after being moved out. 'She wasn't sick but she just passed away, without being bedridden or ill. Some others also died like that. I won't say she died of sickness or old age – I think it was mostly the shock that caused her death because she didn't want to move … she just didn't accept it.'

The damage of apartheid social engineering runs deep. With the sudden and dramatic dislocation of people from their known environment, many men and women, heads of households and spouses alike, became emotionally unstable and were economically disabled. The impact on family life and consequent pressure on that critical social unit proved too much. It resulted in the rise of gangsterism and rampant crime, the scourge that today terrorises these communities.

But the ties that bind people to the city are strong and span the ages. Community leader Leonard Lopes had a dream that was shared by his ex-Tramway Road neighbours. It was a simple dream that gave them hope and optimism after they were forced to leave their homes between 1959 and 1961 when the Group Areas axe fell. The dream went like this: Ilford Road in Sea Point is reconnected with Tramway Road and runs through a townhouse complex built on the site of the park. The laughter of children fills the streets. On Sunday, amid the pealing of church bells, the community attends a service at their church, the Holy Redeemer (in Ilford Road), to praise the Almighty. The ceremony over, they pass on good wishes to each other, gather at table for lunch, and give thanks for their homecoming…

Today, most of the evicted families have been given the go-ahead to return to Tramway Road. Construction work to lay the foundations of new homes has been completed, and if the finance for home loans can be secured, it will be just a matter of time before the dream of Lopes and his original neighbours finally comes true. Sadly, for Mitchell it has come too late. She died recently without seeing her dream come to fruition, and for people like her, the connection with the beloved Mother City is forever severed. But others are slowly but surely restoring it, carrying the hope for a regenerated society.

Photo: Mark Wessels

Remembering our history... Clockwise from left: Ceremonial removal of bones from the Prestwich Street burial site in Green Point. The bones, believed to be from the 1800s, were uncovered during building excavations; archaeologist Gabeba Abrahams-Braybrook at the Slave Lodge in Adderley Street; Bushman diorama removed from display at the Iziko South African Museum after the museum decided to 'archive' the famous hunter-gatherer exhibit 'while its future is reviewed'; the District Six Museum; stone marking the site of the Slave Tree where, for many years, slaves were bought and sold weekly.

Early morning, Khayelitsha.

Turnaround *in* *the* townships

In pockets of the most crime-ridden areas of the Cape Flats,

from Grassy Park to Manenberg, slowly but surely, the tide

is starting to turn against gangsterism, poverty and social

breakdown, towards safer, self-sustaining communities.

And it is taking some of the most unlikely routes.

Left: Domestic and entrepreneurial scenes, Khayelitsha. Above: Police and military anti-crime operation, Cape Flats.

Chapter 8

Turnaround in the townships

The problem of gangsterism has prompted communities to come up with creative ways to engage youngsters, keep them off the street and focus their energy on something constructive and enjoyable.

According to police estimates, there are around 120 gangs on the Cape Flats, with a combined membership of over 100 000. These are tough odds for peace-loving citizens trying to make a difference to their own lives and those of young people caught up in the dangerous world of crime. Yet the problem of gangsterism has prompted communities to come up with creative ways to engage youngsters, keep them off the street and focus their energy on something constructive and enjoyable.

Singing Solution

You wouldn't expect the benign world of song to be an arena for fighting crime, for example. But the Cape Minstrels and Cape Malay Choirs, or *nagtroepe* (night troupes), two of Cape Town's choral institutions, are becoming popular diversions for the young and idle. Thousands of participants gather each year at venues on opposite sides of the Cape Flats for a different kind of fight – to be the best minstrel singing group or Malay choir *nagtroep* of the year.

For the *nagtroepe* competition, troupes gather at the Athlone Stadium at the end of each year before thousands of fans to sing in chorus and put on slick marching displays. No expense is spared in the quest to conquer the coveted object of all the months of preparation, training and jostling for position in the run-up to the finals: the glittering Silver Fez trophy. It is a symbol befitting the origins of the event and has its origins in the headgear adopted by many Cape Malays after it was introduced from Turkey in the late 19th century.

The event is held under the auspices of the Cape Malay Choir Board, whose first contest was held in 1939. That was when author I D du Plessis, who had a life-long interest in Malay culture, teamed up with Springbok rugby star Benny Osler, to organise the first contest at the Cape Town City Hall. There were only six choirs then, compared to the 100 of today. A major feature of the contest is the singing of a traditional song called a *moppie*, or 'comic song', a genre peculiar to the Malay singing troupes. During the competitions, which are very serious affairs (even though the garish neon colours of some costumes don't look it), judging is focused on the best march-past, best timing, best-dressed, and best drum major, to name but a few of the categories. And the judging is not done by any old Sloppy Joe, but by true-blue officers of the South African

Right and following pages: The Cape Malay Choir competition, Athlone Stadium.

The paint and glitter of the Cape Minstrel Carnival, city centre.

COON TROOP CAPTAIN

Soccer game – gun in hand, Cape Flats.

National Defence Force, complete with army battle fatigues and matching berets, observing the military precision of the drills with a steely eye.

Teenagers often join gangs not only out of a need for 'belonging' and for identity, but because there is little else to keep them occupied. The organisers of the *nagtroepe* competition say there is much more to the event than the straightforward singing of cultural songs – there's a particular focus on the youth, who are encouraged to join a *nagtroep* in their area so that they have an interest that will save them from the temptations of crime.

The Cape Malay Choir Board's opposite number, the Cape Minstrel Carnival, holds its annual finals at the Green Point Stadium, an event that takes place over four weeks during the end-of-year festive season. It, too, is concerned that the organisation should be used as a means of providing an alternative for young people to the temptations of drug abuse and gangsterism. Its organisers note that the event is gaining popularity each year and that there's been a keen interest among youngsters in Cape Flats neighbourhoods to take up the saxophone or trumpet or even to beat a drum.

They also point out, and some of the elders lament, that with the gradual and necessary infiltration of younger people into the groups has come a different, more updated, musical style that is starting to change the tenor of the event. Even so, the annual Cape Minstrels street parade held on Tweede Nuwejaar, January 2, is the champion of carnivals, when gaily clad and glitter-faced high-jinxers finally get the chance they've been waiting all year for – to shine. It's an especially long wait for those whose multicoloured satin costumes start being prepared as early as July. As inflation rises year on year, so does the price of a minstrel's costume, which most recently averaged between R100 and R140, for the joy of dancing all day in the sun holding a child's umbrella – and yet there's little in the world to match it, or the Malay choirs, for uniqueness.

Reclaiming the Streets

In other townships, residents have had their own measure of success in addressing local crime, confronting it in a bold and brave way. Bonteheuwel, for example, has over the years been one of the most crime-afflicted townships, but crime dropped dramatically after residents united in a co-operative partnership with regional and local government representatives, which resulted in the installation of closed-circuit television cameras and more visible policing. On Thanksgiving Day, in November 2003, the community came out in force to march through the neigh-bourhood in an anti-crime drive to reclaim the streets they once feared to walk. They stopped at the back of the African Methodist Episcopal Church in Prunus Street and men, women and children watched as a plaque in honour of all those who died due to gang violence was unveiled on a Wall of Remembrance. The plaque bears the names of nine victims. It reads: 'We, the peace-loving people of Bonteheuwel, pay tribute to and remember the innocent victims of violence who tragically lost their lives as a result of the cycle of violence which prevailed over the past few years.' The speeches of church and community leaders and provincial government representatives all focused on the achievements that could be reached when there was unity among communities.

Bonteheuwel also precipitated the almost unthinkable scenario of talks with and between rival gang leaders. Similar anti-crime initiatives are taking root in several other embattled Cape Flats neighbourhoods – with great success.

Cape Flats anti-crime protest, Parliament.

Dancing for Life

Dance for All rehearsals for their annual end-of-year performance, Masikhanye Centre, Gugulethu.

In the sub-economic communities of Gugulethu, Nyanga, Khayelitsha and Athlone, amid the throngs of children and teenagers ambling aimlessly along gravel streets after school, purposeful figures can be seen hurrying to venues such as Gugulethu's Masikhanye Centre. While many children and young adults with nothing to do and no sense of focus get caught up in gangs, crime or drugs, about 200 children aged between eight and 18 make their way eagerly to Dance for All classes every afternoon. They go because they love dancing – be it ballet, jazz, African, Spanish, tap or contemporary. But the experience goes much deeper than that. Dance for All has become an instrument for changing their lives.

It is hard to escape the reality of crime and violence – in fact the career of one of the senior dancers was almost stopped in its tracks when he was shot in the foot by someone trying to mug him. Fortunately the bullet missed the critical bone structure and he has recovered to dance again. There are some whose parents are alcoholics, where home is a violent place, where there is no father figure, where mothers have died and children are left to live with grandparents or other relatives. For all of them, dancing and the caring environment of Dance for All have got them through their difficulties. Many of them claim the teachers and fellow dancers are their family and only support.

Philip Boyd, former Capab (now Cape Town City Ballet) principal dancer, is the founder and artistic director of Dance for All. He is also the energy and driving force that feeds the passion and dedication of the staff and pupils. With his wife, Phyllis Spira, renowned international prima ballerina and icon of South African ballet, Boyd has kept Dance for All going through ups and downs since 1991. During that time, talented young dancers have emerged, not only with top-class training, but with a dream – supported by the poise and self-confidence that are the intangible benefits of Dance for All.

Boyd believes the performing arts are a way of providing a future for many young people in South Africa. Starting a dance company for those whose talent has been nurtured by Dance for All would be a powerful way of continuing the work of the programme. This is where he has set his sights.

They're Crazy about Dance

THANDUMZI MOYAKHE, 20

'Dance for All changed my life. I have self-esteem and respect, I know how to control my emotions. When I wake up in the morning I know I have a purpose and a focus. Dancing keeps me busy, it's saved me… If I was doing nothing, I'd probably be involved in gangs, like some of my old friends in Gugulethu – they're *skollies* [criminals] who rob people.

'I started dancing in 1993 and it's what I want to do with my life. I started choreographing in 2000, so I could express myself more. It's been successful, with my work being staged, sometimes in collaboration with other dance groups. It's my dream to be in a dance company; to dance and carry on choreographing.'

Thamdumzi went on to join the SA Ballet Theatre company in Johannesburg.

NANDIPHA SANDLANA, 23

'I've been dancing with Dance for All since I was 10 years old, now I've been promoted to teacher. I do ballet, jazz, African and contemporary, as well as Spanish dancing, which I started in 1997. I think I love Spanish the most. Dancing is my whole life, I spend all my time here – most of my friends are smoking and drinking and they don't have a focus. Sometimes we go to schools in the townships to tell the children about the programme, to try to attract them to come and dance with us. It keeps them off the street and they have a lot of fun.'

Nandipha has an international sponsor who enables her to be employed by Dance for All.

SILUMKA SILWANA, 16

'If I wasn't dancing, I'd just be at home with nothing to do in the afternoons. Being with Dance for All means a lot to me. I always wanted to dance, since I was six years old, when I got to know African dance. Now I've also grown to like ballet, and contemporary is my favourite. Dancing takes up most of my time and I want to make a career of it. Some of my friends in Langa, who are 15 or 16 years old, are already drinking and robbing people. They call me a *moffie* [effeminate man or boy] because of my dancing, but I just don't listen to them because they're trying to bring me down.

'I wish I could change a lot of things through dancing – like bringing my friends here, stopping crime and other bad things, taking them away from what they're doing. It's my dream to dance here in South Africa and to use dancing to change things.'

AKHONA MAQHINA, 16

'Dancing means everything to me. The people here are my family and friends, some are like my brothers and sisters, I share everything with them. If I didn't dance, I'd probably do drugs or smoke dagga like some of my friends at school. Some of them have even got pregnant. Sometimes people bunk school or they have nothing to do after school, so they get involved in all these things. I've learnt to work hard, come to class regularly and to respect the teachers – but most of all I have fun. Dance keeps me from focusing on other things. My mother died in 2002, she had TB. Four of my friends at school also lost their mothers. When I'm dancing, it really helps because all I think about is that moment. Other times I feel sad. I think of Phyllis as my mother. She and Phil are my family.

'I just focus on dancing, I like contemporary and especially Spanish. And maybe one day I'll be good at ballet.'

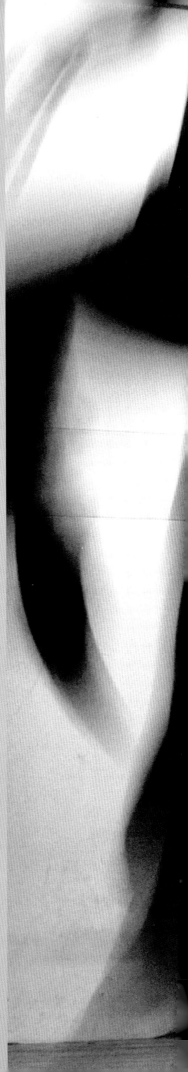

Fashioning *the* future – *today*

With drab, apartheid-era exteriors getting a spruce-up and construction holes being gouged into its historic foundations, Cape Town is having its face lifted and its tummy tucked – for a flood of global investors who have caught on to what may yet be recognised as the discovery destination of the new millennium.

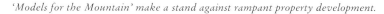

'Models for the Mountain' make a stand against rampant property development.

Chapter 9

Fashioning the future – today

Never in its 350-year history have the prospects for Cape Town looked brighter – and never have the implications of that prosperity been more severe. With increasing investor confidence in this prime location with its accessibility to mountain and sea, Cape Town is experiencing an unprecedented revival of its fortunes as an economic and residential hub.

Anchor tenants who have kept the city ticking over during its leaner economic years are beginning to reap the rewards of their rocky tenure as the city sees its short- and long-term opportunities dramatically improve. They are now providing the base for a run on upmarket residential inner-city development.

The stark, uncompromising architecture that marked the city's concrete heart in earlier years is fast disappearing, replaced by fresh, post-modernist art-deco façades reflecting the optimism of a decade of political change.

Property developers and estate agents are smiling. Small businesses and informal traders can only benefit from the return to a vibrant shopping culture, spawned by business professionals, bankers, ICT fundis, film industry whizzkids and advertising execs.

Foreign investors, undeterred by spiralling price tags for prime local real estate, are vying to be part of a near-miraculous transformation that has been referred to as 'an African success story'. There is strong interest in these inner-city buildings with their plethora of loft-style apartments and superb vistas, which rank equal in breathtaking splendour to the best in the world and are projected to be worth their future investment in gold. The central position of these high-rise developments – virtually in the lap of the omnipresent Table Mountain and only a stone's throw away from the alfresco excitement of Long Street's sidewalk café culture – makes them highly desirable. They are being snapped up as quickly as they are released onto the market.

Having been the Cinderella city in the wings for decades, Cape Town is finally stepping onto centre stage. How her character develops will depend on some defining questions.

Will the city – like Prague after the fall of Communism – be geared mostly towards tourists? Will it exclude most of the local citizens for whom accompanying sky-high prices will be out of reach? Or will it be a unified city, allowing access to economic opportunity for all?

In trying to shape the city's character, its city planners are constantly updating their vision in line with other examples of best-practice urban renewal and development in the world. They are paying as much attention to macro projects as to micro planning. Indeed, the idea of making the city as accessible, interactive and enjoyable for ordinary Capetonians as it is for foreign tourists is fast gaining acceptance across the board.

Urban and Social Renewal

Under the auspices of the Cape Town Partnership – established in 1999 to manage, promote and develop the central city with the aid of business investment – a renewal programme for the Grand Parade, for example, has been undertaken. Like all the CTP programmes, it is based on functional, social upliftment. It involves training and supervising otherwise unemployed homeless people to clean the ablution facilities that serve the historic Parade area, as a first step to transforming it into a more attractive space. The plan is to create a clean and safe environment because the Parade is an important feature of the city.

Cape Town Partnership CEO Andrew Boraine has prioritised a social development programme dealing with homelessness, alcohol abuse, youth at risk (including street children) and substance abuse, as a major focus of CBD concern.

For the longer term, the greater City of Cape Town region has unveiled a draft Integrated Development Plan setting out its vision for achieving a 'healthier, more prosperous and liveable city by 2020' through strategies that incorporate skills development, job creation, building strong communities and improving access and mobility. Two of its major objectives are improving the low-end incomes of working people by 2020 and the drastic reduction of informal settlements through the provision of decent housing for all.

Yet multibillion rand investments to redevelop, rejuvenate and revitalise long-neglected pockets of the city continue to cause people to make pressing demands for a balance between the elitism of luxury apartments and realistic accommodation for those who were historically excluded from living in the city.

Under the East City upgrade plan, 14 buildings are being overhauled by the private sector. The East City includes the Castle, Grand Parade, Granary, District Six Museum, Department of Home Affairs and

Labour buildings, Magistrate's Court, City Hall, Slave Lodge and Parliament. The national government, with its own redevelopment designs for such areas around the country, has bolstered this vision with 20 percent tax breaks for investors, aiming to turn around apartheid's legacy of inner-city decay.

Other developments include the R390-million Icon lifestyle centre which is to rise from the rubble of the old landmark power station on the corner of Lower Long Street and Hans Strijdom Avenue. Comprising three skyscraper tower blocks, it will have 176 apartments with parking bays, shops, restaurants and office space. Well situated virtually next to the V&A Waterfront entrance, it will occupy a 4 000-square-metre site, flanked by the Cape Town International Convention Centre, the Cullinan Hotel and Holiday Inn.

But the development that has the potential to become truly the most iconic in Cape Town – if only for the centuries of sentiment and emotion attached to its name – is the R500-million Mandela Rhodes Place in St George's Mall. Unveiled by its Irish investors as a major vote of confidence in Cape Town as a world-class destination, the plan involves the refurbishment of seven buildings opposite St George's Cathedral into a complex of 163 apartments, a 150-bed five-star hotel, a boutique micro-winery, restaurants and leisure shops.

Investment tax breaks, along with Cape Town's other irresistible attractions, have prompted forecasts of accelerated investment in the city, alongside the more than R6 billion already secured over the last five years. This investment will usher in a period of construction on an unprecedented scale and will change the face of the city that almost never was, forever. Will it be for better or worse in the long run? Pioneer showcase developments such as the V&A Waterfront, and the well-conceived relaunch of St George's Street into a pedestrian mall in the city centre, point to a welcome new approach to urban development that, along with economic concerns, takes serious account of social and environmental issues.

Certainly, the city's caretakers have taken to heart lessons learned from the noxious examples of fume- and smog-cloaked destinations such as Mexico City and Los Angeles. Similarly, they are heeding the interests of the increasingly ecologically conscious tourists who visit Cape Town.

Twenty-first Century Excellence

The pedestrianisation of major thoroughfares is a continuing focus of consideration, as is the feasibility of discouraging the use of family or personal transport in favour of public transport – and especially bicycles – to the city. Another strategy under consideration by the Cape Town Partnership is the creation of appropriate and accessible open public spaces. Following in the footsteps of cities such as Copenhagen, Barcelona and Sydney, Cape Town's top international architects are assessing the quality of its existing public spaces.

Says Andrew Boraine: 'Where usually architects start with a building, we're starting with life, looking at where people go at different times of the year, day and night, weekdays and weekends. We're looking at which spaces are purely functional (such as the railway station) and which can be regarded as social spaces because people choose to be there (such as restaurants and parks). Access to public spaces makes for a democratic city because regardless of whether you have money or not, you can enjoy a space as much as the next person.'

They say the devil is in the detail, and the city is not to be caught napping in its quest for 21st-century excellence. After years of neglect caused by political posturing, infighting and indecision, key tourist attractions such as the Company's Gardens (at the top of Adderley Street) have been upgraded. The area was developed into today's ornamental garden, with trees and shrubs from all corners of the world, after it lost its original purpose of providing produce for Van Riebeeck's refreshment station. When he landed in 1652, an immediate start was made with the planting of vegetables and fruit. Medicinal plants, herbs and ornamental shrubs flourished and the first roses blossomed in 1659. A prized asset as one of the city's few green lung areas (there's a smaller, enclosed 'green lung' tea garden in Burg Street behind the Old Town House on Greenmarket Square), it is within an easy amble of the Iziko South African Museum and its adjoining Planetarium, the Iziko National Art Gallery, the National Library of South Africa, Gardens Synagogue, SA Jewish Museum and Holocaust Centre. It also boasts an aviary, Japanese, herb and rose gardens, and a Victorian koi fish pond.

But this is just one of the many attractions that make the city such a rich cultural-history treasure trove and sought-after developmental hub – it has a compelling mix of past located in the present that fires the imagination of the visitor with a peek into future possibilities.

Cape Town has received international recognition as the most successful business district in South Africa. With an effective urban renewal programme that has helped to reduce the crime rate, spurring hopes for extended retail activity and a 24-hour shopping experience, the city features as one of the top eight international cultural meccas where artists, thinkers and free spirits congregate to fuel a creative vibrancy.

Morning mist envelops the city.

Cape Town has won British and American international travel awards as the best city in the world and the best eat-out city in the world. Yet, with all the hoopla accompanying its status as a newly arrived big-hitter in the global tourism ballpark, an important cautionary has been issued on the need to draw in all the citizens of the Mother City – rich and poor alike – to ensure that its much-needed regeneration and attendant good fortune are sustainable in the long term. The tourism industry, in particular, can play an important role in job creation to draw poor people into the economy.

This vision of inclusivity is keenly supported by the City of Cape Town and the Cape Town Partnership, which have instituted a number of projects to help achieve this goal.

After all, a city is not just a configuration of buildings, streets and shops. A city is also about people.

■ ■ ■

School choir singing outside Parliament.

At a Freedom Day rally in Khayelitsha, a participant proudly shows his only tattoo – of Nelson Mandela.